MELETZIS

PAPADAKIS

NATIONAL MUSEUM

OF ARCHAEOLOGY

ATHENS

NATIONAL MUSEUM OF ARCHAEOLOGY
ATHENS

TEXT AND PHOTOGRAPHS
BY SPYROS MELETZIS
AND HELEN PAPADAKIS

PUBLISHED BY SCHNELL & STEINER · MUNICH & ZURICH
DISTRIBUTION IN GREECE: HELEN PAPADAKIS, ATHENS

All photographs taken by Spyros Meletzis and Helen Papadakis, Athens – Cover design and graphic make-up by Nikos Perakis, Athens – Cover illustrations show the head of the bronze "Youth of Marathon" and remaining pillars of the Parthenon

Translation: Dr. M. Senft-Howie and Theodore A. Papadakis

ISBN 3 7954 0543 2   6 TH EDITION 1970

SOLE DISTRIBUTOR FOR GREECE: HELEN PAPADAKIS, 15 PEFKON ST., ZOGRAPHOU, ATHENS, 625

VOLUME 40/41 IN THE

„GROSSE KUNSTFÜHRER" (ART GUIDES) SERIES PUBLISHED BY DR. HUGO SCHNELL. - © 1963 BY SCHNELL & STEINER, MUNICH AND ZURICH - PRINTED BY THE PUBLISHERS AT WALDSASSEN/OBERPFALZ

THE NATIONAL MUSEUM, ATHENS

INTRODUCTION

This book of particularly striking photos of the most important exhibits in the National Museum at Athens is not intended to be a substitute for a museum catalogue. Its aim is to stimulate the visitor's recollections and to give others an idea of what the Museum contains.

Introductory comments summarise the history of the Museum and indicate its importance. We have tried to give a brief outline of the historical developments pertaining to each monument illustrated, so that the lay visitor will have no difficulty in grasping connections. Serious students of Greek art are referred to the select bibliography at the end.

The history of the National Museum at Athens begins with the history of Modern Greece, i. e. at the end of the Wars of Liberation against Turkey from 1821 to 1829. When the Greeks rose against the Turks, their national consciousness was deeply stirred by their realization of the greatness of their heritage. It was therefore natural that the re-birth of national feeling should be accompanied by the assumption of responsibility for the care of ancient monuments. To collect and maintain them in good condition became one of the noblest aims of the new State.

In 1829 a central museum for finds from all parts of Greece was established at Aegina. At the same time an end was put to haphazard excavation, and the export of works of art was prohibited as far as possible. In 1834 most of the contents of this museum were transferred to the new capital Athens (formerly Nauplia), where they were housed in the Theseion. As finds continued to increase, the collection was accommodated first in Hadrian's Library, then in the Tower of Winds and subsequently in the Propylaea and in other buildings, old and new. The sculptures of the Acropolis found a final home in the museum there. The present National Museum building was presented to the nation in 1874 by Bernadakis. The extension on Patissia Street was completed in 1889 and was enlarged again later.

The new building, erected to the east of the old one, was started in 1925 and completed in 1939, just before the outbreak of the second world war. In order to protect the works of art from the dangers and destructions of the war, all sculptures and other treasures were carefully stored in the basements of the Museum and elsewhere. After the war, the reinstallation and rearrangement of the statues in the Museum's halls took many years.

In 1963, at the time of the first publication of this book, most of the statues were exhibited in temporary places, while a great number of the Museum's halls, as the entire right wing, were closed to the public. The various changes effected gradually for the installation of the statues in their final places and the reopening of almost all the halls (those of the new building are still closed) have necessitated the publication of a new, entirely revised, edition, for the presentation of many works of art, which previously were not exhibited.

Today, the National Museum at Athens contains one of the largest collections of historic Greek monuments. It is distinguished by its comprehensive selection of Cycladic and Mycenaean treasures and, although the archaic, classical and hellenistic periods of Greek art are well represented in the large museums in Rome, Paris, London, Berlin and Munich, they are nowhere displayed in such abundance as in the Museum at Athens. The archaeological setting of each object is, moreover, faithfully preserved, and this is often not the case in other collections. The National Museum of Athens is, therefore, an invaluable source of reference in the field of archaeological research. And, although the main works of Greek art on show elsewhere in Europe are more readily accessible and more widely and copiously publicized, many of the monuments here were unknown to any but the experts. This guide aims, therefore, at introducing the layman to many new works and throws the light of fresh inspiration upon much that, artistically speaking, had become relatively commonplace.

The illustrations do not claim to be exhaustive, nor have they been referred to a common criterion of dignity, being chiefly selected for their vitality and artistic merit. The main emphasis is on archaic and classical sculpture: pottery is only represented by two pieces in the geometric style, so as to confine the material within reasonable limits. The National Museum has a very rich collection of ceramics, unique in his kind which is exhibited in the second floor. This collection, as well as the pottery of the Mycenaean hall, will be presented in a future publication dealing exclusively with the ceramics of the Museum.

Two alternative, and extreme, methods might have been used by the photographers in the task of illustrating works in three dimensions viz. that of austere documentation, characterised by front views and symmetrical lighting or, the eye-catching impressionist approach, complete with spotlight, deep shadow and spectacular angles. In treating each work we have, however, carefully sought for the middle way that would avoid the extremes of lifeless rigidity and dramatic exaggeration.

The order of the illustrations is the same as that in the National Museum, although the order of historical development has generally been followed in the explanatory notes dealing with the various periods.

*

The visit of the Museum begins with the large Mycenaean hall, facing the main entrance. On both sides of this hall are two other halls, the right one dedicated to the Neolithic finds from the Greek mainland and the left one to the Cycladic ones.

NEOLITHIC (3500–2500 B. C.)

AND CHALCOLITHIC AGE (bronze and stone period) (2500–1900 B. C.)

The exhibits of this hall belong to the remotest period of the greek prehistory, a time when the use of metals was not yet known to the early inhabitants of the greek mainland, who used only stones, wood and bones for the confection of their tools, weapons and utensils. The excavations made in Thessaly have brought to light at Dimitri and Sesklo (not far from the town of Volos) two prehistoric citadels, with their palaces and mycenaean beehive tombs. The finds of the neolithic sites consist mainly of hand-made pottery, monochrome with, in relief or engraved, decorations. Other vases are painted and adorned with linear or spiral motives, in various colours: dark red, yellow, black and white. These vases, as well as the figurines in terra cotta or stone, small idols in realistic forms, mainly feminine, are exhibited in this hall.

A find of the Chalcolithic age:

Page 9 Seated Ithyphallic idol in terra cotta.

THE CYCLADES (2500–1900 B. C.)

On the islands in the Aegean Sea the prehistoric period contemporaneous with the Early Minoan civilisation on Crete and the Early Helladic culture on the Greek mainland is known as the "Cycladic" era. The excavations made in the islands of Amorgos, Paros, Naxos, Syros, Siphnos and at the ancient Akropolis of Phylacopi in Milo have brought to light most interesting premycenaean finds, which were found in graves and are now exhibited in the glass-cases of the cycladic hall of the Museum. The objects are mainly vases of clay or marble, of very different shapes, as well as tools, weapons and jewels in bronze or silver. The primitive ceramic is simple or adorned with linear or spiral motives, first engraved and later painted. Among the vases, the sauce-boats and the various pitchers, there are utensils particular to the Cyclads, in the shape of a frier, probably for frying fish, decorated with designs of fish, boats and bound together spirals, which may symbolize the waves. But the most remarkable of the cycladic finds are the primitively symbolic "idols" in marble, tokens of magical conjuration used in the funeral cult, which were found in graves. This multitude of idols, of very different sizes, but mostly small and often of extremely small size, may be divided in four distinct types. The most primitive have a puzzling shape resembling to a violin, then there are those having the form of an unshaped human trunk, with summarily carved arms, and a long headless neck. At last, two types of humanshaped figurines. The first representing the mother-goddess of the Cyclads, with slender arms crossed in front, narrow shoulders, high placed breasts and an elongated and flat head with a prominent nose (the eyes and the mouth were surely painted). The head is posed on a large neck, the feet are joined and the entire body has an elongated and flat shape. The other type has a triangular head, inclined backwards, and a long nose, a stalwart body, almost masculine, with broad, square shoulders and the arms still crossed in front, giving thus to the body the shape of another triangle reaching down to the feet. But the most striking and representative sculptures of the cycladic art are big statues in marble mentioned below.

Page 6 Head of a large Cycladic statue found on the island of Amorgos.

Page 7 Statue of a mother-goddess found on Amorgos, dated circa 2200 B. C.

Page 8 Marble statuette of a harpist found on Keros, dated 2400–2200 B. C.

MYCENAE (1600–1100 B. C.)

Around the middle of the second millennium B. C., as the Minoan court culture of Crete and the Middle Helladic civilisation on the Greek mainland declined, a new warrior civilisation was born on Argolis. Northern immigrants had taken over and modified the Cretan's gay, sophisticated ways of living that had spread to the mainland. When Heinrich Schliemann discovered the massive fortifications in Mycenae and Tiryns in 1876, he also disclosed the birthplace of Homer's heroes.
Within the walls of the Acropolis of Mycenae, not far from the "Lions' Gate", Schliemann discovered, in a circular enclosure, the "Grave Circle", the tombs where, 35 centuries ago, were buried the kings and queens of Mycenae.
Mycenae, "rich in gold", as celebrated by Homer, together with her king, the Atrid Agamemnon, survived as a legend. But the excavations brought to light extraordinary finds, disclosing the reality of a civilization, which remained unknown. A second grave circle, off the Acropolis, comprising 24 tombs from the XVIIth to the XVIth century, was later discovered, in 1952–1955 by J. Papadimitriou. Apart from the royal circles, were also erected, since 1550 till 1200 B. C., imposing vaulted rotundas

to serve as sepulchres for the mycenaean kings. Nine of these tombs, unfortunately already plundered, were discovered around Mycenae. Lastly, in the hills near Mycenae, was found a great number of shaft sepulchres cut into the rock, which constituted the family graves of common mortals.

The royal tombs contained mortuary gold masks, a lot of tiny precious objects, masterpieces of jewelry and ivory sculptures, which were presented as offerings to the deceased. The mycenaeans, who believed that life continued even after death, deposited in the tombs, near the dead, the objects which he liked during his lifetime, as weapons, swords and daggers, in bronze inlaid in gold or silver, golden cups and goblets, decorated with designs in relief, various vases and terra cotta figurines. In the graves of women a considerable amount of jewels: necklaces of golden pearls, of precious stones or of multicolored paste, earrings, golden rings engraved with various scenes of excellent workmanship, caskets covered with golden foils adorned with motives in repoussé and even utensils, as copper cauldrons. All these valuable and interesting finds, revealing a many-sided art and a refined civilization, are exhibited in the 18 first glass-cases of the mycenaean hall. The other 15 cases contain finds discovered in graves of the mycenaean period, in various areas of the Peloponese: Tiryns, Argos, Nauplia, Dendra, Vaphio, Pylos and in Attica. Tombstones, found on the royal sepulchres of the Acropolis of Mycenae, adorned with reliefs are exhibited also in this hall.

Page 1 Gold death-mask of a man, (the "Mask of Agamemnon"), found in a royal tomb, dated 1580–1550 B. C.
Three gold masks from the royal tombs at Mycenae, dated 1580-1550 B. C.
2 Two bronze daggers, inlaid with gold and silver, dated 1600 B. C.
3 Rhyton (libation cup) in the shape of a bull's head in silver with bronze ears, golden horns and a gold rosace on the forehead, dated 1580 B. C.
4/5 Two gold cups found in a tomb at Vapheio, near Sparta, decorated with reliefs depicting a wild bull hunt (4) and domesticated bulls at pasture (5), dated 15 th century B. C.
10/11 Frescoes from the second palace at Tiryns, considerably restored. A boar hunt (10) and women setting off for the chase (11), dated 13th century B. C.
12 Woman's head, circa 1200 B. C.

THE GEOMETRIC STYLE (1050–700 B. C.)

The early period of true Greek art is typified in a large number of austerely styled vases, entirely or partly decorated with geometric patterns. There are also small pictorial bronzes used as votive offerings or buried with the dead. These date from the same period and their composition reveals a systematic structure simplified and formulated by way of geometric designs. A strong sense of order characterises all the objects belonging to this geometric style, in striking contrast to the flowing, sensuous forms of Cretan art.

Page 14 Sepulchral amphora from the Kerameikos Cemetery at the Dipylon Gate, Athens, dated 8th century B. C.
Page 60 Attic sepulchral vase from the Dipylon, dated 750 B. C.

THE ARCHAIC STYLE   (700–490 B. C.)
(The first 7 rooms on the left side of the entrance hall).

About the middle of the 7th century B. C. the Greeks began to produce works in a monumental style. From this period onwards date the first stone temples and the statues of young men (the "Kouroi"), frequently over life-size, that were set up on tombs or in the vicinity of temples. Such nude statues, entirely or partly painted, continued through the 6th century B. C. to form the central theme in contemporary plastic art and, through them, the human figure, and so man himself, was enhanced and translated, beyond the confines of mortality, into regions of fulfilment, where he could lead the life of a hero. The Archaic figures were executed in accordance with a fixed design, based upon a series of vertical and lateral axes on a flat plane, like their Egyptian predecessors. But never before had the human frame been treated on such purely structural lines and with spatial dimension – and never had humans been portrayed with the impressive force of severe but life-like concepts. In the century that was the prelude to classical sculpture, this realistic approach gained in strength and the likenesses lost much of the austere rigidity characteristic of the earliest period, and became less formal. During the later Archaic era too, varied, sensitive, and frequently somewhat decorative, modes of sculptural expression softened the initial rigour. As well as the creative production of statues of young men and girls, carving in relief was extensively practised, both on temples (the pediment, metope and frieze) and on sepulchral pillars and columns.

Two separate categories of sculpture are easily distinguished in Archaic art, the Dorian of the Peloponnese and the Ionian of the islands in the Aegean Sea and of Asia Minor. Doric statuary is solid, bulky, strictly systematic, and massive in construction, whereas the Ionian is softer, making effective play with varied surfaces and with delicate, finely-worked lines that draw the eye upwards. In Attica these two characteristic styles united to produce a Greek art which subsequently gave rise to the Classical works of the Parthenon period.

Page 15 Marble statue dedicated to Artemis by Nicandra of Naxos, found on Delos, dated circa 650 B. C.

13 Bronze helmet and gold mask from Macedonia, dated 6th century B. C. From the Stathatos Collection.

61 Griffon's head from Olympia, dated 6th century B. C.

16 The "Dipylon Head". Attic work, dated circa 610 B. C.

17 Statue of a youth (Kouros) – the "Colossus of Sounion", – found near the Temple of Poseidon at Cape Sounion, dated circa 600 B. C.

18 Ionian statue of a youth, found on the island of Milo, dated circa 550 B. C.

19 Winged "Nike" found in the Sanctuary of Apollo, Delos. Ionian work, dated circa 550 B. C.

20 Youth with discus, fragment of a gravestone stele found at the Dipylon, Athens. Attic work, dated circa 560 B. C.

21 Statue of a youth found at Volomandra. Attic work, dated circa 550 B. C.

55 Bronze statuette of a horseman. Doric work, dated circa 550 B. C.

23 Head of a Doric statue found at Ptoïon, dated circa 540 B. C.

24/25 Doric statue of a youth found in the Sanctuary of Apollo, Ptoïon, dated circa 540 B. C.

64/65 Large bronze statue of Apollo, found in 1959 in the Piraeus, dated circa 530–520 B. C.

28 The Anavyssos Kouros. Attic work, dated circa 520 B. C.

22 The stele of Aristion. Attic work, dated circa 510 B. C.

26 Hoplite in relief. Attic work, dated circa 510 B. C.

27 Head of a warrior, found near the Temple of Aphaia on Aegina. Doric work, dated circa 490 B. C.

29 Base of an Attic statue, dated circa 510 B. C.

THE CLASSICAL STYLE (480–350 B. C.)

This style, too, is not limited to any fixed period, but rather represents a stage in the historical development of the arts which reached its zenith when the Parthenon was built and when Phidias and Polycleitos (circa 438 B. C.) were executing their masterly works.

The famous "Archaic Smile" disappeared somewhere between the 6th and 5th centuries B. C. when artistic expression became simpler, concise and more fluent. The over-refinements of the late Archaic style were followed by sober, monumental and altogether grander aesthetic forms, the "severe style", which lasted from 480 to 460 B. C. Whereas in Archaic sculpture the limb muscles appear uniformly flexed, a rhythmic contrast of tensed and relaxed posture now makes itself apparent: the human form takes on a realistic mobility and "lives". From the contrasting interplay of leg muscle, and from asymmetries in the line of the shoulder and hip and in the pivoting motions of the human frame, a positive and exemplary technique in the delineation of the human body emerges – the "counterpoise". Variations in physical stresses and strains as portrayed by the classical treatment of muscular balance in the human body, are also directly identified with man's struggle against fate. A new awareness informs these statues: man, now fully conscious of the transitory nature of his existence, seeks to endure the burden of his own limitations with heroic fortitude. Neither before nor since has art succeeded in taking the nature of man so seriously and, at the same time, in so enhancing, distilling and, finally, deifying it. These statues of youths, men and women may thus represent mortal heroes, or the Immortal Gods, without either losing anything of their earthly character nor detracting from their enduring supernatural qualities. The key to classical art lies in this harmoniously changing equipoise between the contrasts of rest and movement, tension and relaxation, dignity and vivacity, humanity and the gods. By the 4th century B. C., the expression of movement has acquired a richer refinement. The mood has changed; subtler sentiments are now revealed in statues and in the figures on gravestone stelae; the simple heroic poise is gradually overlaid. Works by Praxiteles and Skopas mark the finale of this phase, of the "aesthetic style".

42 Gravestone stele, circa 400 B. C.

43 Athena of Varvakeion. A Roman copy in marble of the statue of Athena Parthenos (39'–4" high) by Phidias (438 B. C.). The original, in gold and ivory, stood in the Parthenon.

44/45 Attic gravestone stele of Hegeso, circa 400 B. C.

54 Small bronze statue of Zeus casting a thunderbolt, circa 450 B. C.

46 Head of Athena, marble copy of an original from the end of the 5th century.

47 Head of Hera, found at Heraion near Argos, circa 420 B. C.

48/49 Youth wearing victor's wreath, the "Diadumenos". A Roman copy in marble after a bronze original by Polycleitos, dated 420 B. C. Copy from 1st century A. D.

50/51 Hermes of Andros. A Roman copy in marble after an original from the 4th century.

52 Statue of goat-footed Pan. A Roman copy of an original from the 4th century.

53 Relief dedicated to the Nymphs, found in a cave on Mount Pentelicus, 4th century.

68/69 Sculptures from the temple of Asclepios at Epidauros, dated 380 B. C.

71 Head of Hygeia, possibly by Skopas, found at Tegea, Arcadia, circa 350 B. C.

70 Head of Ariadne, dated 4th century.

72 Bronze woman's head. Copy of an original from the 4th century.

75 Head of Asclepios, found on Amorgos, 4th century.

86/87 Bronze statue of Athena by Cephisodotos, found in Piraeus; dated circa 375 B. C.

34/37 Youth of Antikythera, original, in bronze, circa 340 B. C.

66/67 Youth of Marathon, original, in bronze, circa 350 B. C.

THE HELLENISTIC STYLE (340–30 B. C.)

During the three centuries from Alexander to Augustus, a "Hellenistic" culture developed and Greek civilisation, and art, predominated in all the lands bordering the Mediterranean Sea. Sculptors no longer sought to portray realistic phenomena but turned for inspiration to things of the spirit. Dynamism, passion, mood and feeling were now the favoured themes. The range of hellenistic expression extended from decorative grace to pathos, from the lovable to brutality, and from elegance to sheer ugliness. The plastic artist, moreover, preferred to obtain his effects by means of blended, mobile contours and impressive light and shadow contrasts. Over wide areas art began to burst the bonds of religious worship and though the resulting emphasis on the more striking and unique traits in nature entailed some sacrifice of robust vitality, this was compensated by virtuosity in characterisation. To this period, then, belongs the most imposing imagery, in the form of portraiture.

Page 74 Bronze head of a boxer, found at Olympia, circa 340 B. C.

78 Head of a woman, found at Lerna, Argolis, dated 4th century.

79 Votive relief from a sanctuary at Oropos, Attica, dated 4th century.

88 Mask of tragedy in bronze, dated 4th century.

77 Bronze head of a philosopher, found in the sea off Antikythera, dated 3rd century.

73 Marble statue of Themis by Chairestratos, found at Ramnus, in Attica. Dated 3rd century.

80 Statue of a child, found at Polydrosson, dated 3rd century.

81 Statue of a child with a dog, found in Asia Minor. Copy from an original of the 3rd century.

62/63 Jockey of Artemision, bronze statue found in the sea near Cape Artemision, dated 2nd century.

76 Bronze head of a man, found on Delos, circa 100 B. C.

82 Poseidon of Melos, circa 140 B. C.

83 Aphrodite, Eros and Pan group found on Delos, dated 2nd century B. C.

84/85 The dancing "Horae" from the theatre of Dionysos, dated 1st century B. C.

BIBLIOGRAPHY

General

Pausanias: "Periegesis" (Itinerary of Greece), "Loeb Series" ed. by W. H. S. Jones, H. A. Ormerod and R. E. Wycherley (1918-35)
"Bildatlas der Klassischen Welt" (An Atlas of the Classical World), published by A. A. M. van der Heyden. German edition published by the Gütersloher Verlagshaus Gerd Mohn; 1960
Ernst Buschor: "Von griechischer Kunst" (On Greek Art). Selected writings, published by Piper Verlag, München; 1956
G. Rodenwaldt: "Die Kunst der Antike" (The Art of Antiquity), published by Propyläen-Kunstgeschichte, 3, Berlin; 4 th edition 1944
G. M. A. Richter: "A Handbook of Greek Art", The Phaidon Press, London; 1959
Thomas Zacharias: "Kleine Kunstgeschichte der Antiken Welt" (A Brief History of Art in the Ancient World), published by Schnell & Steiner, München; 1962
Fischer-Lexikon: "Bildende Kunst" I. (Dictionary of the Fine Arts – Vol. I), published by W. H. Schuchhardt, Fischer-Bücherei, Frankfurt; 1960

Mycenae

F. Matz: "Kreta, Mykene, Troia" (Crete, Mycenae and Troy), published by Gustav Kilpper, Stuttgart; 1957
Marinatos & Hirmer: "Kreta, Mykene" (Crete and Mycenae), published by Hirmer Verlag, München; 1959

Greek Sculpture

Ernst Buschor: "Frühgriechische Jünglinge" (Early Greek Youths) published by Piper Verlag, München; 1950
Ernst Buschor: "Die Plastik der Griechen" (Greek Sculpture), published by Hirmer Verlag, Berlin; 1936
Lullies & Hirmer: "Griechische Plastik" (Greek Sculpture), published by Hirmer Verlag, München; 1956
J. Charbonneaux: "Les Bronzes Grecs" (Greek Bronzes), published by Presses Universitaires, Paris; 1958
W. H. Schuchhardt: "Die Epochen der Griechischen Plastik" (Epoches in Greek Sculpture), published by Bruno Grimm Verlag, Baden-Baden; 1959
A. A. Papayannopoulos-Palaios: "The archeology of Piraeus" (in greek) published in the Archeological review "Polemon", volume 7 (1959/62), Athens

Vase Painting

Ernst Buschor: "Griechische Vasen" (Greek Vases), published by Piper Verlag, München 1940
Arias & Hirmer: "Tausend Jahre griechische Vasenkunst" (A Thousand Years of Greek Vases), published by Hirmer Verlag, München; 1960

Museum Catalogue

Papaspyridi: "Guide du Musée National", Marbres, Bronzes et Vases Athènes (Guide to the Marbles, Bronzes and Vases in the National Museum, Athens); 1927
V. Stais: "Collection Mycénienne" (Mycenaean Collection), Guide of the National Museum of Athens; 1909
V. Stais: "Marbres et Bronzes du Musée National" (Marbles and Bronzes of the National Museum), Athens; 1910
S. Karouzou: "National Archaeological Museum: Collection of Sculpture", Athens; 1968
A. Sakellariou – G. A. Papathanasopoulos: "National Archaeological Museum. I. Prehistoric Collections", Athens; 1964

LIST OF ILLUSTRATIONS

hinted by a girdle and toes just emerging under the long, unplaited, dress. The triangular face and the hair in tresses on both sides, forming another two triangles. Height 5 ft 10". Dated 650 B. C. Cat. No. 1.

16   Head from statue of a youth, from the Dipylon Gate, Athens; the "Dipylon Head", in marble, height approx. 17 inches, dated circa 610 B. C. Cat. No. 3372.

17   Colossal marble statue of a youth (Kouros), found near the temple of Poseidon, Cape Sounion and called the "Colossus of Sounion". It is one of the oldest and biggest "Kouroi" preserved in good condition and the type of the archaic "Kouros" or "Apollo". Most interesting is the stylized coiffure, in small snailshaped tresses on the forehead, as well as the large arched eyes and the big ears. The legs of this strong colossus are enormous. Height 10 ft. Dated 600 B. C. Cat. No. 2720.

18   Statue of a youth (Kouros), from Melos, Ionian, Naxian marble, height approx. 7 ft., dated 550 B. C. Cat. No. 1558.
More slightly built than the other Kouroi, this statue shows its insular character. The surface of the marble has been sensibly eroded by wind and rain, loosing many details.

19   Winged "Nike" from Apollo's Sanctuary, Delos; Ionian, in marble, height approx. 3ft. 3 inches, dated 550 B. C. Cat. No. 21.
This archaic Nike was probably an acroterium on the ancient temple of Artemis. She had big wings on her back and small wings at her feet. The torso is seen in front view, while her legs, parted and kneeling, are in profile. The long tunique, uncovering the right knee, is falling, in folds between the legs, down to the ground. The statue was based on this tunique, the legs not touching the ground, giving thus the impression of a winged race. The invention of the winged Nikes is ascribed to Archermos, ancient sculptor of Chios.

20   Fragment of a sepulchral stele, representing in relief and in profile the head of a youth, winner at the Games, holding a disc behind his head. It was found at the Dipylon. The modelling is splendid and the profile very expressive. A beautiful attic work of a great but unknown sculptor, in Parian marble. Height 13 inches 2", dated 560 B. C. Cat. No. 38.

21   Kouros from Volomandra; Attic, in marble, height approx. 6 ft., dated 550 B. C. Cat. No. 1906.

22   The stele of Aristion, by Aristocles, from Velanideza; Attic, in Pentelic marble, height approx. 8 ft., dated 510 B. C. Cat. No. 29.
This archaic stele, tall and narrow, crowned originally with a palmette, represents the type of the funeral attic steles of the 6th century. This low relief is remarkable for the perfection and delicacy of its modelling. Traces of the colors are still visible. An inscription engraved on the base names the warrior represented and the sculptor.

23   Head of a statue from Ptoïon, Doric, in limestone, height approx. 13 inches, dated 540 B. C. Cat. No. 15.

24 + 25 Kouros from Apollo's Sanctuary, Ptoïon; Doric, in marble, height approx. 4 ft. 11 inches, dated 540 B. C.
The style of this Kouros is much more advanced than the preceding ones. The arms are more free and slightly bent at the elbows. The figure is more expressive and keeps smiling. The coiffure is most carefully arranged, in curls and symmetrical spirals framing the forehead. Cat. No. 12.

26   Running Hoplite in relief, from Athens. Parian marble, height approx. 3 ft. 3 inches, dated 510 B. C.
This remarkable sepulchral stele represents a naked warrior wearing an enormous helmet on his head and running with both arms posed on his chest. His torso is twisted and his head is bent backwards, giving the impression that he is exhausted and is rendering his last breath. Attic work. Cat. No. 1959.

27   Head of a warrior found (together with 5 other heads of the same style) near the Temple of Aphaia on Aegina; in marble, height approx. 1 ft., dated circa 490 B. C. Cat. No. 1933.

28   The Anavyssos Kouros. Sepulchral statue of a youth, found in 1936 at Anabyssos, attic in Parian marble, height approx. 6 ft., dated circa 520 B. C.
This Kouros represents young warrior Kroisos, full of life and vigour, who died prematurely on the battlefield. The statue stood on a three-tiered base, of which

only the middle one was preserved, bearing in front the following distich: "Stand and mourn by the tomb of dead Kroisos, whom furious Ares snatched away from among the warriors in the front rank." The athletic structure of this youth and his powerful muscles distinguish him from the other Kouroi. Remains of red paint are visible on the hair and the eyes, as well as a reddishbrown patine on the whole body. Cat. No. 3851.

29   Reliefs from the base of a statue, showing a ball-game, wrestling match and youths setting a dog against a cat; Attic, in Pentelic marble, height approx. 13 inches, dated 510 B. C.
This base, built into the wall of Themistocles at Kerameikos was found in 1922. The 14 young athletes composing these three low reliefs are full of life and movement, while the modelling is meticulous in all its details. Visible yet is the red paint with which the background was painted. Cat. No. 3476.

30   Fragment of a circular low relief representing the beautiful greek profile, figure and neck, of a woman, probably of goddess Aphrodite. The hair at the back is bound up in a veil and falls down to the neck. A hole near the ear served to attach the disc to a stele or as a wall ornament, and also, probably, to fix a metal diadem around the front. Found on Melos in 1937. Ionic, in Parian marble, height approx. 13 inches, dated 460 B. C. Cat. No. 3990.

31   Votife relief of a youth crowning himself with a wreath won at the athletic games. The range of holes on the head shows where the metal wreath was attached. Found in 1915 at Cape Sounion, near the temple of Athena. Attic, in Parian marble, height approx. 2 ft. 4 inches, dated 470 B. C. Cat. No. 3344.

32   Gravestone stele of a youth, found in Thessaly; Doric, in marble, height approx. 5 ft. 11 inches, dated 440 B. C. Cat. No. 741.
Gravestone stele of a youth, found in Thespiai, Boeotia; in marble, height approx. 7 ft. 4 inches, dated 440 B. C. Cat. No. 742.

33   Great votive relief found in 1859 at Eleusis. This magnificent low relief is one of the most beautiful masterpieces of greek sculpture. It represents the two goddesses honored at Eleusis: Demeter, goddess of Agriculture and her daughter Persephone-Kore, together with, young Triptolemos, son of the king of Eleusis and a favourite of Demeter. On the left, Demeter is portrayed in a long doric chiton falling in vertical folds, her hair short and wavy. With a solemn and grave expression, she holds a sceptre in her left hand, while handing with her right some ears of corn to Triptolemos, which were in gold or bronze, but are missing.
Triptolemos, in the centre, almost naked (he holds carelessly a cloak thrown on his right shoulder) gazes at the symbolic ears of corn, being fully aware of the importance of the mission entrusted to him, to travel around the world on his winged chariot drawn by serpents and spread out the cultivation of the wonderful corn to mankind.
To the right, Persephone, radiating a youthful grace and wearing an ionian linnen chiton and the himation, is placing on the head of the elected youth a wreath in gold or bronze (also missing) while holding in her left hand her particular symbol, the long torch reaching to the ground.
The deeply religious character of this composition and its masterly modelling prove that this relief is the work of a great sculptor. Attic, in Pentelic marble, height approx. 8 ft., dated 440 B. C. Cat. No. 126.

34 + 37   The youth of Anticythera. The boat transporting this beautiful bronze statue, together with many other art pieces, from Piraeus to Rome, sunk south of the Cape of Malea. Two thousand years later, in 1900, this statue was found at the bottom of the sea, near the island of Anticythera. Broken into many pieces, it was remarkably well restored and now it is almost intact. The powerful and athletic structure of this youthful and naked body is reminiscent of the style of the school of Polycleitos.
The head with short and curled hair, the face with harmonious and attractive features, the lively, fierce and colored eyes gazing at a distant object, are reminiscent of Hermes of Praxiteles. But who was the person portrayed by this statue and what was he holding in his raised right hand? Was he a god, Hermes, or a hero, Perseus holding Meduse's head, or Paris offering the golden apple to Aphrodite, or simply an athlete holding a ball? And who was the sculptor who created it? All these questions have vainly preoccupied the archeologues, no adequate answer being given as yet. Height approx. 6 ft. 5 inches, dated 340 B. C. Cat. No. 13396.

35 + 36 Poseidon of Artemision. Bronze statue, found in the sea off Cape Artemision, Euboea. Height approx. 6 ft. 11 inches, span of the outstretched arms 7 ft. Dated 460 B. C.

This masterpiece represents Poseidon hurling the trident, he is holding, almost horizontaly, in his right hand. The left arm outstretched to direct the throw and balance the body, the head turned to the left towards the target, the feet apart and hardly touching the ground, this is the characteristic position of the javelot throwers. Remarkable is the modelling of this athletic body, full of vigour and movement, as well as the way it is balanced on a minimum surface.

The coiffure is very carefully arranged, according to the archaic style of this period: two pigtails, crossed at the back, are disposed around the head over a fringe of waved hair adorning the forehead. The beard and the long moustaches are well carved. The features of the face are fine and harmonious. The inlaid eyes are missing. The entire statue radiates a divine majesty and vigour.

Due to its long stay in the sea, the bronze has taken a green patina. This statue of the preclassical period must have, undoubtedly, been made by a famous but unknown sculptor. It is ascribed either to Kalamis, the great Athenian master of this period or to the Aeginetian Onatas. It is probable that this statue was dedicated to Poseidon after the victorious sea-battle of Salamis. Cat. No. 15161.

38 Great marble Lecythos, found in Athens in 1873. Height approx. 8 ft. 8 inches, dated 420 B. C.

This big funeral vase represents in relief, in the centre, Hermes, the conductor ot souls (Psychopompos), holding by the hand a young woman, Myrrine (her name is engraved over her head). He is leading her to the banks of river Acheron, whence Charon will take her by boat to the Kingdom of Hades. Cat. No. 4485.

39 Gravestone stele from the Piraeus; Attic, in Pentelic marble, height approx. 4 ft. 9 inches, dated 410 B. C.

This stele, crowned with a pediment and two pilasters on both sides is broken diagonally. Its left part is missing. It represents two standing figures, a man and a woman, looking with deep grief at a woman seated on the left, the deceased. The expression of the faces and the beautiful folds of the drapery are remarkable. Cat. No. 716.

40 Dionysos and actors, votive relief from the Piraeus; in marble; height approx. 22 inches, dated 400 B. C. Cat. No. 1500.

The Rape of the Nymph Basile, by Echelos, votive relief: Attic, in Pentelic marble, height approx. 2 ft. 6 inches, dated 400 B. C. Cat. No. 1783.

41 Gravestone stele of a youth, found at Salamis; Attic, in Pentelic marble, height approx. 3 ft. 7 inches, dated 420 B. C. Cat. No. 715.

42 Sepulchral stele, found at Kerameikos, Athens, in 1870. A high relief portraying a very touching farewell scene. A young girl stands to the right and presses the hand of her seated mother, the deceased, with an expression of calm grief. The father, standing in the centre, is looking tenderly at his daughter. Height approx. 4 ft. 11 inches, dated 400 B. C. Cat. No. 717.

43 "Athena of Varvakeion", found in Athens, in 1880, near the Lyceum of this name. Roman copy of the statue of Athena Parthenos (approx. 39 ft. 4 inches high, in gold and ivory, in 438 B. C.) by Phidias for the Parthenon. This masterpiece of Greek sculpture has only been preserved in this bad copy in Pentelic marble, approx. 3 ft. 5 inches high.

There are, however, some differences in details from the description given by Pausanias (1, 24, 6). Instead of the two griffons on Athena's helmet, the copyist has carved two Pegasus. Besides, Athena was holding the spear on her left hand and not the shield, which rested at her feet. The copyist has also neglected all the ornaments in relief which were on the shield, the base and the sandals, and has only carved a Gorgon's head on the shield. This work, however, is valuable, because it is one of the surviving reproductions of Phidias' masterpiece. Cat. No. 129.

44 + 45 Funeral Stele of Hegisso, daughter of Proxenos and the wife of Koroibos, from the Kerameikos Cemetery; Attic, in Pentelic marble, approx. height 4 ft. 11 inches, dated 400 B. C. The sepulchral stele has the form of a small temple, a pediment adorned with acroteria on its three angles and pilasters on the sides, framing the two figures in relief, as was customary at the end of the 5th century.

Hegisso, whose name is inscribed on the horizontal transon over her head, is seated on the right, in profile, on a chair. She wears a fine chiton, a light himation richly draped and a transparent veil on her hair. Her feet rest on a stool. In front of her, standing in profile, her maidservant, wearing a simple tunic, holds out to her a jewellery case. Hegisso has taken out of it a necklace, which surely was painted. An expression of deep sorrow is depicted on the faces. This is one of the masterpieces of the attic art of this period. Cat. No. 3624.

46 Head of Athena in marble, wearing a corinthian helmet adorned with two heads of ram in relief, found in the Agora of Athens. This head belonged to a copy of a statue of the 5th century. Height 1 ft. 4. Dated 2nd century B. C. Cat. No. 3004.

47 Head of a woman in marble, belonging probably to a statue of Hera, found in the temple of Heraion, near Argos. The harmony and the finesse of the features and the perfect modelling denote that it is the work of a great master, perhaps of the famous argian sculptor Polycleitos or of his school. Height 10 inches, dated 420 B. C. Cat. No. 1571.

48 + 49 The "Diadumenos", a Roman copy in marble of Polycleitos' vanished bronze original. Found on Delos, height approx. 6 ft. 2 inches. Original dated 420 B. C., copy from 1st century A. D.
This young athlete, victor at the games, wearing a broad ribbon on his forehead, is raising his arms to girdle himself with the wreath he won. The perfection of this harmonious body justifies the renown of Polycleitos, who was the most famous, after Phidias, sculptor of the 5th century. The trunk, the quiver and the himation, which serve as a support, have been added by the copyist. Cat. No. 1826.

50 + 51 "Hermes of Andros". Statue of Hermes, from Andros, Roman copy of Empire period, after an original dated 4th century B. C. Height approx. 6 ft. 8 inches. This statue in Parian marble, whose legs have been restored, was found, together with a woman's statue, near a tomb. A snake, an infernal symbol, is rolled up around a trunk, which serves as a support. This is surely a copy of a bronze original of Praxiteles' school. Cat. No. 218.

52 Statue of goat-footed Pan with cloak and syrinx, Roman copy, found at Sparta, of an original dated 4th century B. C. Height approx. 2 ft. 11 inches. Cat. No. 252.

53 Relief dedicated to the Nymphs, found in a cave on Mount Pentelicus; Attic, in marble, height approx. 2 ft. 4 inches, dated 4th century B. C. Cat. No. 4466.

54, 55 + 57 Three bronze statuettes from Carapanos' Collection. Found by M. Carapanos in 1875–1877 during the excavations made at Dodona, near Ianinna, Epirus. The oracle of Dodona was the oldest of Greece and its sanctuary was dedicated to Zeus and Dione.

54 Bronze statuette of Zeus casting a thunderbolt, from the Sanctuary of Zeus at Dodona. Height 4·8 inches, dated 450 B. C. Cat. No. 16546.

55 Bronze statuette of a horseman, found in the Sanctuary of Zeus at Dodona; Doric, approx. 4 inches high, dated 550 B. C. The two parts composing it, the rider and the horse, were found separetely. Cat. No. 16547 + 27.

56 Bronze statuette of Athena Promachos, from the Acropolis, Athens. Dated circa 480 B. C. Wearing a helmet with a high panache, in chiton and himation, Athena Promachos (fighting at the first rank) is depicted here as she fights brandishing her protruded spear in her right hand, while defending herself with the shield in her left. (The two weapons have not been found). An archaic inscription is engraved on the base. Height 11 inches. Cat. No. 6447.

57 Bronze statuette of a woman with a dove, 10·4 inches high, dated 460 B. C. This statuette portrays a goddess, Dione, honored at Dodona, wearing a large tunic folded up at the waist. It is composed of two pieces joined by pegs. Cat. No. 540.

58 Male head in bronze, found on the Acropolis. Life-size. This warrior's head of archaic style, with features very finely designed, well carved beard and moustaches, was undoubtedly the original work of a great Aeginetian sculptor. A helmet covered originally the hair, which emerged under it in fine laces framing the forehead. The eyes were filled with a white and glittering material. Dated 490 B. C. Cat. No. 6446.

59 Bronze head of Zeus, from Olympia; early 5th century B. C.
Height 6·8 inches. This archaic work belonged to a statuette of Zeus. The coiffure is very stylised with 2 ranges of curls framing the forehead, a diadem on

the head and a chignon on the neck. The beard is pointed and the eyes, of another colored material, were inlaid. Cat. No. 6440.

60   Great Vase of geometric style. Found in 1891 at the Dipylon Gate, Athens, height approx. 4 ft. 1 inch: dated 750 B. C.
This Dipylon vase was posed on a tomb as a funeral monument. The designs in reddish-brown represent a funeral procession. In the centre is the burial chariot and on both sides the lamentations, expressed by a procession of small figures with raised arms and hands posed on their heads. Below is a procession of chariots. All these motifs are of a very primitive design, adorned by rosaces, birds, svastikas and a frieze of meanders on the border. Cat. No. 806.

61   Griffon's head from Olympia, in bronze, dated 6th century B. C.
Griffon protome (sculpture of head and neck) which adorned a cauldron on a tripod. This extremely decorative though imaginary monster was often used to ornate various objects. The whole surface of its neck is finelly engraved with scales and other spiral designs. Cat. No. 6159.

62 + 63   The Jockey of Artemision, bronze figure found in the sea off Cape Artemision, N. E. of Euboia island, in 1929; dated 2nd century B. C.
This excellent work, which survived thanks to the shipwreck of the cargo transporting it, probably to Constantinople, represents a lively young rider galloping on his horse (which is missing). The legs parted and the arms in movement, he still holds part of the reins. He wears a short chiton attached on his left shoulder. All the muscles are in tension. The face is very expressive and shows the ardour and effort exerted by the young cavalier. The eyes, which were inlaid and of another material, are missing. The legs are nude, except for the spurs attached to the heels with thongs, encircling the ankles and feet (see detail). Cat. No. 15177.

64 + 65   Big bronze statue of Apollo (in detail also), found by chance in 1959 by workmen digging in a street in Piraeus. Height 6 ft. 4 inches, dated circa 530–520 B. C.
This Apollo or Kouros is quite different from other archaic Kouroi. He has the right leg forward instead of the left and his hair is combed differently. In his left hand he was holding a bow and in his right probably a phiale (a sort of flat saucer without handle or base). This Kouros is the oldest of the hollow cast bronze statues which were preserved and is attributed to a Peloponnesian sculptor.

66 + 67   "Youth of Marathon", bronze original, found at the bottom of the sea, off the coast of Marathon, in 1925, height approx. 4 ft. 3 inches; dated 350 B. C.
The natural and gracious position of this youth, with his left arm bent at the elbow and the palm outstretched, while his right arm is raised in the air, suggests that the artist has tried to fix in the bronze a passing, though graceful, movement of his model.
Many suppositions have been put forward about the identity of the missing objects he once held on his left palm and in his raised right hand, but none is fully convincing. The short and curling hair is encircled by a ribbon, knotted at the back and with a forward-curving tongue at the top. The eyes are inset and composed of a hard and colored material. The youth's gaze is directed towards the object he once held on his left palm. This charming statue, whose creator is unknown, presents great affinities with the works of Praxiteles. It is surely the work of a great attic sculptor. Cat. No. 15118.

68 + 69   Sculptures in Pentelic marble which adorned the temple of Asclepios at Epidauros. Probably works of Timotheos. On the west pediment of this temple is represented the fight of the Amazons. No. 136. In the centre, Penthesile, the Queen of the Amazons, is portrayed on horseback, in short tunic, raising her right arm and hurling her spear against the enemy. It is a figure full of movement, with perfect draperies, though markedly mutilated. Height 3 ft. No. 157. One of the two figures which adorned the acroteria of the west pediment. A Nereid or Aura is represented riding on a very mutilated horse. Fine drapery. Height 2 ft. 7. Dated circa 380 B. C. Cat. No. 136 and 157.

70   Marble head of a woman, found in 1878, to the south of the Acropolis, near Dionysos' Theater.
The head, slightly reclining rested on her right arm, the traces of which are still visible on the right ear. It belonged probably to a statue of abandoned Ariadne. Above the dionysian ribbon encircling her head, she was wearing a diadem adorned by bronze rosaces. There were holes below the ears to attach it. A beautiful work ascribed to Skopas. Height 1 ft. 3., 4th century B. C. Cat. No. 182.

71   Head of the Goddess Hygeia (the Goddess of Health), from Tegea, Arcadia,
      probably by Skopas; Parian marble, 11·2 inches high, dated 350 B. C.
      This head of great classical beauty, with noble and harmonious features, was
      found in 1900, east of the temple of Alea Athena. The architect of this temple
      was the famous sculptor Skopas of Paros, who has designed and probably exe-
      cuted the well known pediments of the temple. In the temple, beside the cult
      statue of Athena, were the statues of Asclepios and Hygeia, both works of
      Skopas. Most naturally it was presumed that this beautiful head, undoubtedly
      the work of a great master, belonged to this Hygeia, whose body was missing.
      Pausanias, however, who is giving these informations (VIII, 47, 1), adds that
      these statues were made of Pentelic marble (!). Consequently, this head might
      not, after all, represent Hygeia. The coiffure is remarkable. The hair, parted in
      the middle, is combed backwards over the ears and, at the back, upwards into
      a sort of curled crown held by a band. This head had been stolen in 1916 from
      the Museum of Tegea, but after 9 years it was found again and placed in the
      Museum of Athens. Cat. No. 3602.

72   Woman's head in bronze, made after the casting of a bronze head (found at
      Herculanum and now exhibited in the Museum of Naples), which was a roman
      copy of a statue of the 4th century B. C. The features are harmonious and the
      beautiful coiffure is crowned with a thick tress, encircling the head. Height 1 ft.
      1. Cat. No. 15187.

73   Big marble statue of Themis, found in 1890 in her temple at Ramnus, in Attica.
      The goddess of justice was probably holding in her right hand, which is missing,
      a balance in bronze. The statue has a divine majesty. It is the work of Chaires-
      tratos, as indicated by an inscription on his base. Height 7 ft. 4., 3rd century
      B. C. Cat. No. 231.

74   Bronze head of a pugilist, found in 1880 at Olympia; 11·2 inches high, dated
      340 B. C. This powerful and sombre looking face, with a flat nose, short and
      untidily curled hair, an abundant beard and half-closed eyes (inserted and made
      of a different material) is certainly the realistic portrait of a boxer. An olive
      wreath, from which only two small leaves are left, surrounds the head. It is,
      undoubtedly, the portrait of a victor at the games, who had the right to erect his
      statue (the body has not been found) in the place of honor in the Altis, the sanct-
      uary of Zeus at Olympia, among the other victors. It is presumed that this
      vigourous portrait represents Satyros, a renowned boxer. It is ascribed to the
      athenian sculptor Silanion. Cat. No. 6439.

75   Marble head of Asclepios, god of medicine, found on Amorgos (Cyclades). Height
      1 ft. 2. 4th century B. C. Cat. No. 323.

76   Head of a man, bronze in dark green patina, found in the ancient Palestra of
      Delos, in 1912. Height approx. 13 inches; dated 100 B. C. The coloured eyes,
      marvellously well preserved (only the bronze lashes are missing) give to this very
      expressive face a gloomy expression. This head depicting a famous at his time
      man, was set in a dressed statue, which was not found. Cat. No. 14612.

77   Head of a philosopher in bronze, found in the sea off Antikythera; 11·6 inches
      high, dated 3rd century B. C. This beautiful head belonging to a life-size statue,
      parts of which were also found (the right arm, the left hand holding a stick and
      the sandalled feet), was the realistic portrait of an elderly philosopher. Its long
      stay at the bottom of the sea has eroded this head, especially the inlaid eyes.
      Cat. No. 13400

78   Head of a woman, found at Lerna, on Argolis; in marble, dated 4th century B. C.
      This head of attic style was detached from a funeral stele in high relief. Height
      2 ft. 4. Cat. No. 188.

79   Votive relief from the Sanctuary of Amphiaraos at Oropos, Attica; in marble,
      dated 4th century B. C.
      This relief, in form of a small temple, represents successively three very interes-
      ting scenes. A young man, Archinos, in the centre, is bitten, during his sleep, by
      a serpent. The god-prophet Amphiaraos reveals to him, in a dream, the remedy for
      his cure. To the left, Archinos is healed by a doctor according to the oracle. To
      the right, Archinos, standing, dedicates in gratitude to Amphiaraos this votive
      relief, represented also in the background. Cat. No. 3369.

80 Marble statue of a child playing with a goose, found at Polydrosson, ancient Lilaea (Phokis) in 1853; dated 3rd century B. C. Cat. No. 2772

81 Statue of a child, in a large riding hood, hardly standing on his feet. He tenderly hugs in his arms a small dog. Found in 1922 in Asia Minor. Height 2 ft. 4. Copy of an original of the 3rd century B. C. Cat. No. 3485.

82 Poseidon of Melos. Colossal statue of Poseidon in Parian marble, found on Melos in 1877. The God of the sea holds majestically the trident in his right hand. At his feet a dolphin, his symbol. Height 7 ft. 2. Dated 140 B. C. Cat. No. 235.

83 Aphrodite, Eros and Pan. Group found on Delos, in the establishment of the Poseidoniastes of Berytos (Beirut). Parian marble. Aphrodite surprised, completely naked, by Pan, who tries to pull her by the arm, defends herself with her sandal in her right hand. A winged Eros over her left shoulder is pushing back the goat-footed god. The contrast between the gracious and smiling beauty of Aphrodite and the bestial ugliness of Pan is striking. Height 4 ft. 4. End of the 2nd century B. C. Cat. No. 3335.

84 + 85 Reliefs found in 1862 in the sanctuary of Dionysos in Athens. These reliefs represent two dancers or the dancing Horae (Hours) Karpo and Thallo, wearing a light and transparent himation, whose draperies wave in the wind. Height 3 ft. 8 and 3 ft. 4, width 2 ft. 1. Dated 1st century B. C. Cat. No. 260 and 259.

Appendix: The following pieces of sculpture in bronze, were found in Piraeus, during work on the roads. They represent the most important finds of recent times.

86 + 87 Big statue of Athena in bronze (and detail). Height 7 ft. 10, dated circa 375 B. C.

Athena standing in a long tunic, crowned with a big crested helmet with representations of Griffons and, on her breast, the aegis with the Gorgoneion and adornments of curled snakes, was holding in her left hand her spear and her shield, resting on the ground, and in her outstretched right hand, as offering it, a victory. Athena was represented thus as coming from Olympus, in full battledress to offer the victory to the city of Piraeus. (Some archaeologists think she was rather holding a phiale.) This original work is ascribed to Cephissodotos, father of Praxiteles. It must have been in the sanctuary of Zeus Soter and Athena Sotera (Savior) in Piraeus.

88 Mask of tragedy in bronze, height approx. 17 inches, dated 4th century B. C. This mask must have belonged to the cult of Dionysos, whose sanctuary must have been near the sanctuary of Zeus and Athena. Now in the Archaeological Museum of the Piraeus.

Disposition of the statues and pieces of art
in the various rooms of the Museum

Illustration page	Work No	Room No	Illustration page	Work No	Room No
1	624, 253, 259, 254	4	42	717	18
2	394, 395	4	43	129	20
3	384	4	44/45	3624	18
4/5	1758, 1759	4	46	3004	28
6	3909	6	47	1571	17
7	3978	6	48/49	1826	21
8	3908	6	50/51	218	21
9	5894	5	52	252	34
10/11	5878, 5882	4	53	4466	34
12	4575	4	54	16546	36
13		32	55	16547-27	36
14	804	7	56	6447	37
15	1	7	57	540	36
16	3372	8	58	6446	37
17	2720	8	59	6440	37
18	1558	9	60	806	44
19	21	9	61	6159	44
20	38	10	62/63	15177	35
21	1906	10	64/65		43
22	29	11	66/67	15118	35
23	15	8	68/69	136, 157	22
24/25	12	13	70	182	28
26	1959	12	71	3602	28
27	1933	12	72	15187	28
28	3851	13	73	231	29
29	3476	13	74	6439	30
30	3990	14	75	323	28
31	3344	14	76	14612	30
32	741	14	77	13400	30
32	742	15	78	188	24
33	126	15	79	3369	26
34/37	13396	28	80	2772	30
35/36	15161	15	81	3485	30
38	4485	16	82	235	30
39	716	16	83	3335	30
40	1500, 1783	17	84	260	30
41	715	16	85	259	30

Musée National d'Athènes
Plan du rez-de-chaussée

National Museum of Athens
Plan of the ground-floor

Nationalmuseum Athen
Grundriß des Erdgeschosses

41   42   43   44   47

37   36   45   46

40   35

Cour
Court
Hof

34

Cour
Court
Hof

38

39

16   17   18   21   22   23   24

20   19   25   28

15

Jardin
Garden
Garten

5   4   6

Cour du Musée
Epigraphique

Court of the
Epigraphic
Museum

Hof des
Inschriften-
Museums

26   29

14

27

10

13   9   30

3

31

11   8   7   33   32

12   1   2A

2

Plan of the National Museum

1 Entrance   2A Exhibition of mouldings   3 Entrance-hall   4 Mycenaean hall   5 Neolithic finds   6 Cycladic finds   7-13 Archaic Art   14 Early 5th century   15 Early 5th century, Poseidon's hall   16-20 Classical Art, 5th century. Gravestone stelae and votive reliefs   21 Diadumenos' hall   22 Sculptures from the sanctuary of Asclepios at Epidauros   23-24 Gravestone stelae, 4th century   25-27 Votive reliefs, 4th century   28 Youth of Anticythera's hall   29 Themis' room, 3d century   30 Hellenistic Art   32 Stathatos Collection   34 Votive sculptures, Hall leading to the new building of the museum   35 Stairs to the upper floor. Ceramic collection   36 Carapanos Collection, Dodona   37 Bronze Collection   38-47 Rooms closed for rearrangement

Abbreviations   Abréviations   Abbreviazioni   Abkürzungen

a. Chr. = ante Christum natum (before – avant – vor – Jesus Christus)

p. Chr. = post Christum natum (after – après – dopo – nach – Jesus Christus)

s. = saeculum (century – siècle – secolo – Jahrhundert)

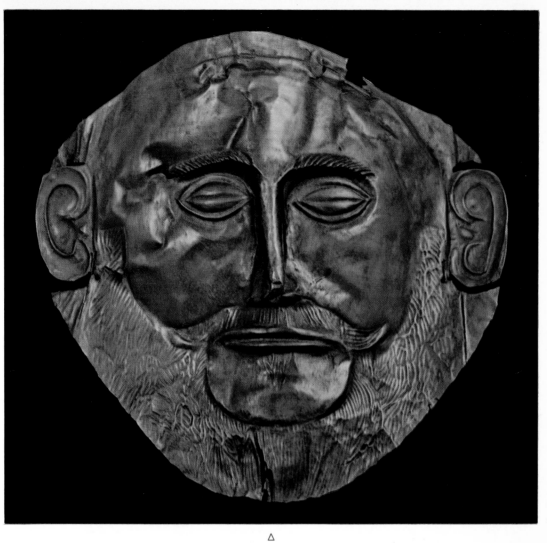

△

624

1580 – 1550 a. Chr.

Mycenaean Gold Masks	Masques en or mycéniens	Gold-Masken aus Mykenä
253	259	254

394-395
1600 a. Chr.

Daggers from the
Royal tombs of
Mycenae
Poignards prove-
nant des tombes
Royales de My-
cènes
Dolche aus den
Königsgräbern
in Mykenä

◁

▷

384 1580 a. Chr.

Mycenaean
Bull's Head
Tête de taureau
de Mycènes
Stierkopf aus My-
kenä

1758   XV. s. a. Chr.

Two sides of a gold cup from the tomb at Vaphio. The hunting of wild bulls
Les deux côtés d'un gobelet en or, trouvé dans la tombe à tholos de Vaphio.
Scène de chasse aux taureaux sauvages
Zwei Seiten eines Goldbechers aus einem Grab in Vaphio. Jagd wilder Stiere

1759   XV. s. a. Chr.

Two sides of a gold cup from the tomb at Vaphio. The tamed bulls
Les deux côtés d'un gobelet en or, trouvé dans la tombe à tholos de Vaphio.
La vie des taureaux apprivoisés
Zwei Seiten eines Goldbechers aus einem Grab in Vaphio. Die wilden Stiere
sind gebändigt

3909   2400 – 2200 a. Chr.

◁ Head of a large cycladic statue, from Amorgos
Amorgos. Tête d'une grande statue cycladique
Kopf einer Monumentalstatue aus Amorgos

3978   2200 – 2000 a. Chr.

Female statue from Amorgos
Statue feminine, Amorgos   ▷
Weibliche Statue aus Amorgos

3908   2400 – 2200 a. Chr.

Keros (near Amorgos). Statuette of a musicien
Keros (près d'Amorgos). Statuette d'un musicien
Statue eines Harfenspielers aus Keros bei Amorgos

5894   2000 a. Chr.

Terra cotta of an idol from Thessaly. Chalcolithic period
Idole assise en terre cuite trouvée en Thessalie. Période chalcolithique
Terrakotta Idol der Jungsteinzeit aus Thessalien

5878   1300 – 1200 a. Chr.

Fragment of wall-painting from Tiryns. Boar hunt
Fresque du second palais de Tirynthe. Scène de chasse
Freskomalerei aus Tiryns. Jagdszene

5882   1300 – 1200 a. Chr.

Fragment of wall-painting from Tiryns
Fresque du second palais de Tirynthe
Freskomalerei aus Tiryns

1200 a. Chr.

Female head of limestone from Mycenae
Tête feminine calcaire de Mycènes
Weiblicher Kopf aus Mykenä, Kalkstein

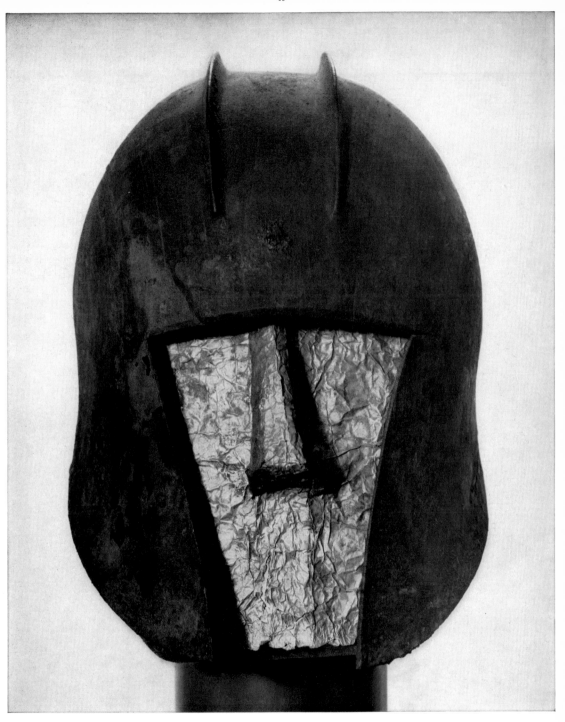

VI. s. a. Chr.
Bronze helmet and gold mask
Casque en bronze et masque funéraire en or
Bronzehelm und Goldmaske

804 800 a. Chr.

Large sepulchral amphora of geometric style found in Dipylon

Grande amphore funéraire de style géométrique du Dipylon

Große Grabamphora in geometrischem Stil vom Dipylon in Athen

◁

▷

650 a. Chr.

„Nicandra".
Marble statue dedicated to Artemis by Nicandra of Naxos

„Nicandra".
Statue féminine, dédiée à Artémis par Nicandra de Naxos. Dédicace gravée sur le côté gauche

„Nikandra".
Marmorstatue, der Artemis in Delos von Nikandra aus Naxos geweiht. Separat die auf der linken Seite eingravierte Inschrift

3372   600 a. Chr.

◁ The „Dipylon Head"
La „tête du Dipylon"
Der „Dipylon-Kopf"

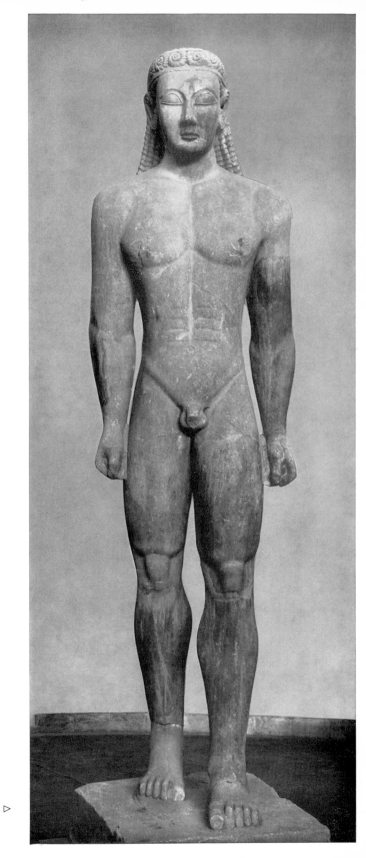

2720   600 a. Chr.

Colossal Kouros from the Temple
of Poseidon at Sounion

Kouros Colossal trouvé au Temple
de Poseidon au Sounion   ▷

Überlebensgroßer Kouros aus dem
Poseidontempel in Sunion

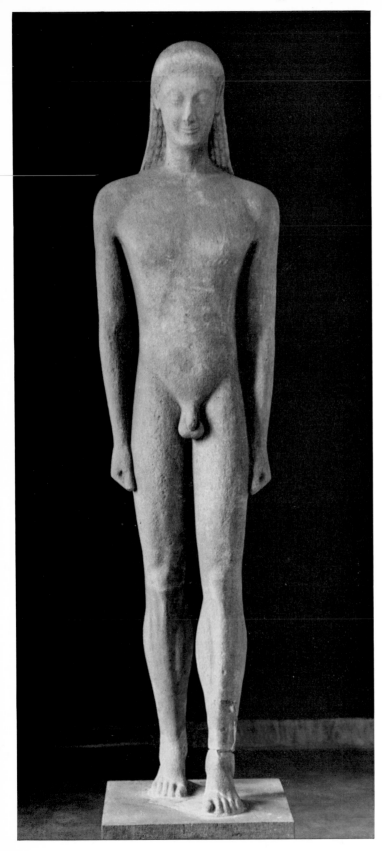

1558   550 a. Chr.
Statue of a youth (Kouros) from Milos
Statue d'un Kouros de Milo
Kouros von Melos

21   550 a. Chr.

Winged   Nike
found at Delos
Niké ailée trou
vée à Délos
Geflügelte Nike
aus Delos

38   560 a. Chr.

Fragment of a grave stele found at the Dipylon
Fragment d'une stèle funéraire trouvé au Dipylon
Bruchstück einer Grabstele vom Dipylon

1906   550 a. Chr.

Statue of a Kouros from Volomandra - Attica
Kouros de Volomandra, Attique
Kouros von Volomandra, Attika

29   510 a. Chr.

The stele of Aristion by Aristocles
Stèle funéraire d'Aristion, œuvre
d'Aristoclès
Grabstele des Aristion von Aristokles

15   540 a. Chr.

Head of a statue from Ptoïon
Tête d'une statue de Ptoïon
Kopf einer Statue aus Ptoïon

12   540 a. Chr.
Kouros from the Sanctuary of Apollo at Ptoïon
Kouros du Sanctuaire d'Apollon au Ptoïon
Kouros aus dem Heiligtum des Apollo in Ptoïon

1933   500 a. Chr.
Warrior's head from the Temple of Aphaia in Aigina
Tête de guerrier du temple d'Aphaia à Egine
Kopf eines Kriegers aus dem Aphäatempel in Ägina

1959   510 a. Chr.
Relief of a running hoplite
Bas-relief d'un hoplitodrome
Relief eines Hopliten

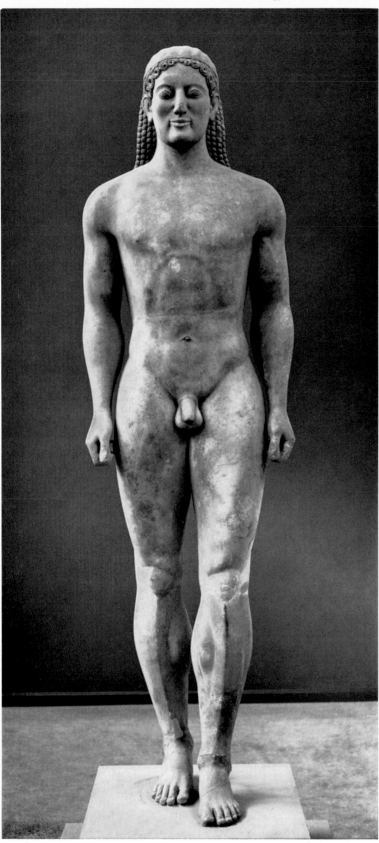

3851   530 a. Chr.
The Anavyssos Kouros
Kouros trouvé à Anavyssos
Kouros aus Anavyssos

◁

▷

3476   510 a. Chr.
Palaestra Scenes on the base of
a Kouros Statue
Base de la statue d´un Kouros
avec des scènes de Palestre
Reliefs von einer Statuenbasis

3990   460 a. Chr.

Circular slab with a female head
Bas-relief circulaire avec une tête féminine
Relieftondo mit weiblichem Kopf

3344   470 a. Chr.
Votive relief found at Sounion
Relief votif d'un jeune homme, trouvé au cap Sounion
Votivrelief aus Sunion

33

◁ 741   440 a. Chr.
Grave stele of a youth from Thessaly
Stèle funéraire d'un jeune homme trouvée en Thessalie
Grabstele eines Jünglings aus Thessalien

◁ 742   440 a. Chr.
Grave relief of a youth from Bœotia
Stèle funéraire d'un jeune homme. Béotie
Grabstele eines Jünglings aus Böotien

△

126   440 a. Chr.
Great votive relief found at Eleusis
Grand relief votif trouvé à Eleusis
Großes Votivrelief aus Eleusis

15161   460 a. Chr.

Poseidon of Artemision
Poseidon d'Artémision
Poseidon von Artemision

13396   340 a. Chr.

◁   The youth of Anticythera
L' Ephèbe d' Anticythère
Der Jüngling von Antikythera

15161 460 a. Chr.

Poseidon of Ar-
temision

Poseidon d´Ar-
témision

Poseidon von Ar-
temision

◁

▷

13396 340 a. Chr.

The youth of An-
ticythera

L´Ephèbe d´ An-
ticythère

Der Jüngling von
Antikythera

◁ 4485   420 a. Chr.

Great marble Lecythos of Myrrine

Grand Lécythe en marbre de Myrrine

Große Lekythos aus Marmor, aus Myrrine

716   410 a. Chr.   ▷

Grave-stele from Piraeus

Stèle funéraire du Pirée

Grabstele vom Piräus

1500   400 a. Chr.

◁ Votive relief found in Piraeus
Relief votif trouvé au Pirée
Votivrelief vom Piräus

△

715   420 a. Chr.

Tombstone of a youth from Salamis
Stèle funéraire d'un jeune homme de Salamine
Grabstele eines Jünglings aus Salamis

1783   400 a. Chr.

◁ Attic votive relief
Relief votif attique
Attisches Votivrelief

717   400 a. Chr.

Grave Relief   Stèle funéraire   Grabstele

New results of research / Nouveaux results scientifiques
Neue Forschungsergebnisse / Risultati scientifici nuovi

Illustration page / Illustration page / Bildtext Seite / Illustrazione pagina	instead of / au lieu de / anstatt / invece	corr. / corr. / korr. / corr.
14	800	750
17	600	610
27	500	490
28	530	520
48	440	420
56	500	480
59	550	490
65	476	525
64/65	Zeus Soter	Apollo
72	found at Perinthos	Copy from the Naples Museum
72	trouvée a Perinthe	Copie, se trouvant au Musée de Naples
72	aus Perinthos	Kopie im National-museum zu Neapel
72	Perinthos	Copia nel Museo Nazionale di Napoli

129   Orig. 438 a. Chr.

Athena of Varvakeion. Roman copy of Athena Parthenos by Phidias

L'Athéna du Varvakeion. Imitation romaine de l'Athéna Parthénos de Phidias

Die Athene von Varvakeion. Römische Kopie der „Athena Parthenos" von Phidias

3624   400 a. Chr.

Funeral relief of Hegisso   Stèle funéraire d'Hégéso   Grabstele der Hegeso

3004   Orig. 400 a. Chr.
Head of Athena
Tête d'Athéna
Kopf der Athene

1571   420 a. Chr.
Head of Hera from Argos
Tête d'Héra trouvée à Argos
Kopf der Hera aus Argos

48

1826   Orig. 440

„The Diadoume-
nos" found at De-
los. Roman copy

Statue du „Dia-
dumène" - Délos
Copie romaine

Statue des „Dia-
dumenos" aus
Delos, römische
Marmorkopie
eines Bronzeori-
ginals von
Polyklet

218   Orig. IV. s. a. Chr.

„Hermes of Andros", Roman copy
L'„Hermès d'Andros", Copie romaine
Der „Hermes von Andros", römische Kopie

252   Orig. IV. s. a. Chr.

Pan wrapped in a mantle and
holding the syrinx. Roman copy.
Found at Sparta

Pan sérieux, en manteau, tenant
la syrinx. Copie romaine. Trouvé
à Sparte

Pan, in einen Mantel gehüllt,
mit Hirtenflöte (Syrinx), Römische Kopie. Gefunden in Sparta

4466   IV. s. a. Chr.
Attic relief dedicated to the Nymphs
Relief attique dédié aux Nymphes
Attisches Relief aus einer Nymphengrotte

16546   450 a. Chr.
Bronze statuette of Zeus holding the thunderbolt
Statuette en bronze de Jupiter lançant la foudre
Blitzschleudernder Zeus, Bronze-Statuette

16547   550 a. Chr.

Bronze statuette of a horseman
Statuette d'un cavalier en bronze
Bronze-Statuette eines Reiters

◁ 6447   500 a. Chr.

Bronze statuette of
Athena Promachos
from the Acropolis

Statuette en bronze
d´ Athéna Promachos
de l´Acropole

Bronze-Statuette der
Athena Promachos
von der Akropolis

460 a. Chr.   ▷

Bronze statuette of a
woman holding a
dove

Statuette en bronze
de femme tenant une
colombe

Bronze-Statuette
eines Mädchens mit
Taube

6446   490 a. Chr.
Bronze head from the Acropolis
Tête en bronze. Acropole
Bronzekopf von der Akropolis

6440   550 a. Chr.

Bronze head of Zeus. Olympia
Tête en bronze de Zeus. Olympie
Bronzekopf des Zeus aus Olympia

806   750 a. Chr.

Dipylon vase of geometric style. Ceramicos
Vase de style géométrique du Dipylon
Grabgefäß vom Dipylon

6159   VI. s. a. Chr.
Bronze Griffon from Olympia
Tête de griffon en bronze — Olympie
Greifenkopf aus Olympia

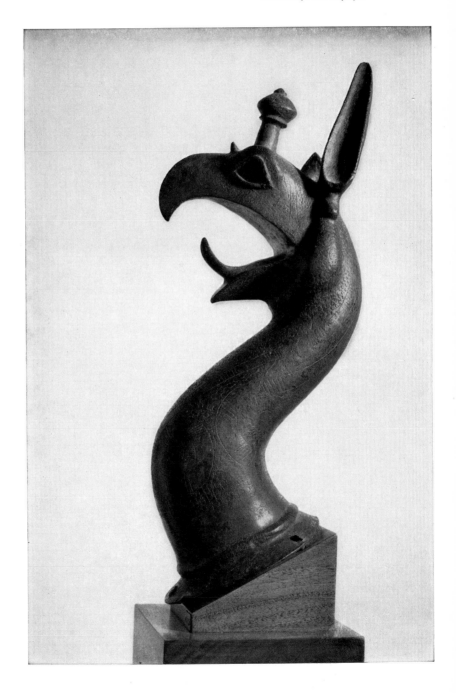

15177   II. s. a. Chr.

The Jockey of Artemision
Le Jockey d'Artémision
Der Reiterknabe von Artemision

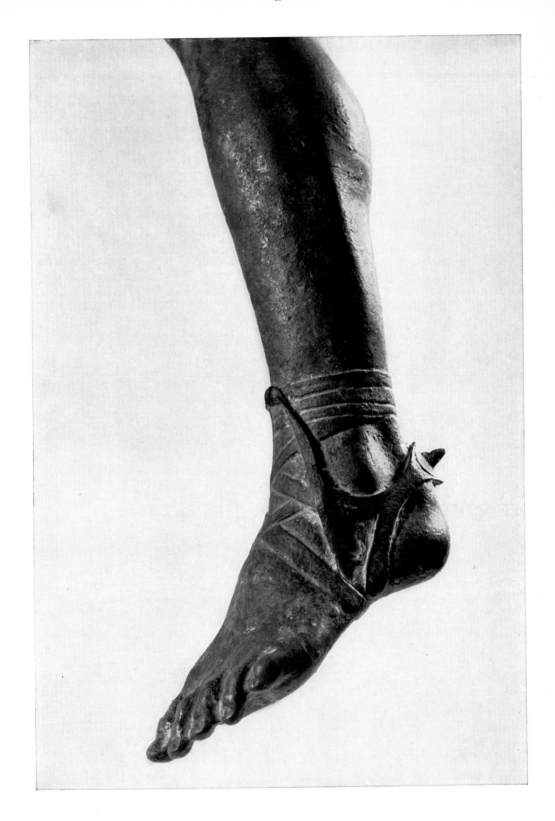

Head of the Bronze Zeus Statue
Tête de la Statue en bronze de Zeus
Kopf der Bronze-Statue des Zeus

476 a. Chr.

Bronze Zeus Soter found at Piraeus
Zeus Sôter en bronze trouvé au Pirée
Bronze-Statue des Zeus Soter vom Piräus

15118 350 a. Chr.

The youth of Marathon

L′ Ephèbe de Marathon

Der Jüngling von Marathon

136   380 a. Chr.
Sculpture from the temple ot Asclepios at Epidauros
Sculpture qui ornait le temple d'Asclépios à Epidaure
Marmorskulptur aus dem Tempel des Asklepios in Epidauros

157   380 a. Chr.
Sculpture from the temple of Asclepios at Epidauros
Sculpture qui ornait le temple d'Asclépios à Epidaure
Marmorskulptur aus dem Tempel des Asklepios in Epidauros

182   IV. s. a. Chr.

Head of Ariadne

Tête d'Ariane

Kopf der Ariadne

3602   350 a. Chr.

Head of Hygia found in Tegea
Tête d'Hygie trouvée à Tégéa
Kopf der Göttin Hygieia aus Tegea

15187   Orig. IV. s. a. Chr.
Bronze woman's head found at Perinthos (Thrace). Roman copy
Tête de femme en bronze, trouvée à Périnthe (Thrace). Copie romaine
Bronze-Kopf einer Frau aus Perinthos (Thrazien). Römische Kopie

231   III. s. a. Chr.

Themis from Rhamnonte
(Attica), by Chairestratos

Thémis de Rhamnonte
(Attique), oeuvre de Chairestratos

Themis aus Rhamnonte
(Attika), Werk von
Chairestratos

6439   340 a. Chr.
Bronze head of a pugilist from Olympia
Tête en bronze d'un pugiliste. Olympie
Kopf eines Faustkämpfers aus Bronze. Olympia

323   IV. s. a. Chr.

Head of Asclepios from Amorgos
Tête d'Asclépios trouvée à Amorgos
Marmorkopf des Asklepios aus Amorgos

14612   100 a. Chr.
Head of a man found in Delos
Portrait d'un homme trouvé à Délos
Kopf eines Mannes, aus Delos

13400   III. s. a. Chr.

Head of a philosopher
Portrait d'un philosophe
Kopf eines Philosophen

188　　　IV. s. a. Chr.

Head of a woman found at Lerna
Tête d'une femme trouvée à Lerne
Kopf einer Frau aus Lerna

3369   IV. s. a. Chr.

Votive relief from the sanctuary of Amphiaraous at Oropos
Bas-relief trouvé au sanctuaire d'Amphiaraos à Oropos
Votivrelief aus dem Heiligtum des Amphiaraos in Oropos. Attika

2772 III. s.

Statue of a
child with a
goose

Statue d'un
enfant avec
l'oie

Statue eines
Kindes mit
Gans

3485
Orig. III. s.a.Chr.

Statue of a Child
with a dog
Statue d'un
enfant tenant un
chien
Statue eines
Kindes mit Hund
aus Kleinasien

235　140 a. Chr.　　　Poseidon of Melos　　　Poseidon de Milo　　　Poseidon von Mil[

a. Chr.

odite,
and Pan
Delos

odite, Eros et Pan, groupe trouvé à Délos

Aphrodite, Eros und Pan, aus Delos

260   I. s. a. C

The dancing Horae f
the theatre of Diony
Athens

Les "Heures" dans
du théâtre de Dionys
Athènes

Die tanzenden „Hor
aus dem Theater
Dionysos. Athen

59   I. s. a. Chr.

The dancing Horae from
the theatre of Dionysos.
Athens

Les "Heures" dansant,
du théâtre de Dionysos.
Athènes

Die tanzenden "Horen"
aus dem Theater des
Dionysos. Athen

PIRAEUS ARCHAEO-
LOGY MUSEUM

MUSÉE ARCHÉOLO-
GIQUE DU PIRÉE

ARCHÄOLOGISCHES
MUSEUM PIRÄUS

IV.   s. a. Chr.

Bronze statue of Athena
Statue en bronze d'Athéna
Bronzestatue der Athene

Head of Athena wearing the helmet with its crest
Tête d'Athéna portant le casque intact
Kopf der Athene mit dem Helm

IV. s. a. Chr.
Bronze mask, like those actors held in tragedies
Masque en bronze, comme ceux tenus par les tragédiens
Tragödien-Maske aus Bronze